The Spirit of the Thunderbird

DONALD M. ANTOINE

Belleville, Ontario, Canada

THE SPIRIT OF THE THUNDERBIRD
Copyright © 2012, Donald Antoine

All Rights Reserved. No part of this publication may be reproduced, stored in a retrieval system or transmitted in any form or by any means—electronic, mechanical, photocopy, recording or any other— except for brief quotations in printed reviews, without the prior permission of the author.

ISBN: 978-1-55452-782-3
LSI Edition: 978-1-55452-783-0
E-book ISBN: 978-1-55452-784-7

Cataloguing data available from Library and Archives Canada

To order additional copies, visit:
www.essencebookstore.com

For more information, please contact:
Donald Antoine
P.O. Box 285
Sharbot Lake, ON K0H 2P0

Epic Press is an imprint of *Essence Publishing,* a Christian Book Publisher dedicated to furthering the work of Christ through the written word. For more information, contact:
20 Hanna Court, Belleville, Ontario, Canada K8P 5J2
Phone: 1-800-238-6376 • Fax: (613) 962-3055
Email: info@essence-publishing.com
Web site: www.essence-publishing.com

Printed in Canada
by
Epic Press

TABLE OF CONTENTS

Introduction 7
1. Native History 9
2. History of the Iroquois Nation 18
3. The Colonization of Quebec, 1608–1763 24
4. History of French Iroquois War Started
    by Champlain 25
5. The Huron Nation 37
6. Algonquian North Woodland Nation 43
7. The Chippewas and Mississaugas of
    Great Lake Superior 51
8. Pontiac: War Chief of the Ottawas 53
9. The Story of a Shawnee Chief: Tecumseh 56
10. Major General Sir Isaac Brock 61

INTRODUCTION

I returned to school after the war on January 1, 1946, and one of the history lessons was from *The Plains of Abraham*, by James Oliver Curwood. I had an immediate interest in Curwood. I visited the old Toronto library, which only had one of his books, and you had to stay there to read it. They told me that he had written many books but there were few published copies of some of them. He wrote thirty-two books, and it took me fifty years to complete my collection of them.

Upon retiring in Sharbot Lake, I joined the local historical society to write about the local people and their ancestors. I soon found out that an oral history beyond the third generation is useless to historians.

I then started collecting war history books and writing for the newspapers and Legion books. My articles were well received by the newspapers, and when high school students were going to visit Vimy, I taught them about the battle of the Somme and the battle of Vimy Ridge.

I then started a book on the United Empire Loyalists and one family. I had the book published. About eight years ago I started collecting native history books and wrote this book.

chapter 1

NATIVE HISTORY

The first Canadian explorer, John S. Cabot, in 1497 explored Newfoundland and the area from Cape Breton to the Gaspe. His report of great fishing in these areas brought the Spanish, the French, and the Portuguese. They made many fish-curing and -drying camps along these shores and traded with the Micmacs.

Next came Jacques Cartier in 1534. As he approached the Gaspe many canoes of Micmacs came out to meet him, loaded with things to trade. He proceeded to the mouth of the St. Lawrence, meeting a large number of Iroquois fishing for mackerel. A year later he came to the New World, up the St. Lawrence to Stadacona (now Quebec City) and on to Hochelaga (now Montreal). There was an estimated population of about 1,000 Iroquois in each of these areas and many villages in between.

He returned in 1541 with Roberval to commence settlement in New France. There were large plantations of corn throughout this area.

In 1603 Samuel de Champlain made a voyage up the St. Lawrence. The Iroquois who had inhabited the region in Cartier's time had disappeared. He found about 500 natives in each of Stadacona and Hochelaga, made up of a mixture of Algonquins, Hurons, and Montagnais.

Sometime between Cartier's time in 1541 and Champlain's time in 1603, a period of approximately sixty-six years, the Iroquois had moved south and north of Lake Ontario, between Lake Champlain and Niagara.

The Iroquois Confederacy was composed of Mohawks, Oneidas, Onondagas, Cayugas, and Senecas. The Tuscaroras (Iroquois speaking) joined them to make up the Six Nations. The Tuscaroras were driven out of North Carolina in 1713.

The Iroquois were hostile to the other nations: the Algonquins, the Tobaccos and the Neutrals of southwest Ontario, the Hurons on Georgian Bay, and the Ottawas on Manitoulin Island. These nations had to take their furs up the French River to Lake Nipissing and down the Ottawa River to trade with the Algonquians and the French at the trading post at Three Rivers. The Hurons were big traders with the Algonquins, trading corn, squash, and beans for wild rice and hides for making clothes. History shows that this route and trade had been going on for many years.

In 1648, the Iroquois started to eliminate their enemies. They depopulated the Neutrals and the Tobacco tribes. On then to the Hurons, by taking one village at a time. The Ottawas of Manitoulin Island fled across Georgian Bay to what is now Green Bay, and the Algonquins fled north of Lake Nippissing into Cree country.

Five hundred Iroquois patrolled and occupied the Ottawa River for many years in the 1650s. A few Hurons who were still in their old Georgian Bay area and some Algonquins and Ottawas were able to avoid the Iroquois and get their furs to the trading post at Three Rivers via the St. Maurice River.

In 1660 the Algonquin captured an Iroquois, who told the French at Montreal that 800 Iroquois were across the river from Montreal waiting for 500 Iroquois on the Ottawa River and that they planned to attack Montreal and drive the French out of Canada.

Adam Dollard des Ormeaux and sixteen of his comrades, along with some Algonquins and Hurons, fortified an old fort at Long Sault on the Ottawa River to stop the Iroquois from getting to Montreal. This small group fought the Iroquois for five days and nights, giving up their lives. Their courage so impressed the Iroquois that they decided not to attack the fortified city of Montreal and retreated to their bases north and south of Lake Ontario. The Iroquois left unoccupied all the lands they had taken, but they still occupied all the area north of Lake Ontario.

The Mississaugas and the Chippewas were part of the great nation of Ojibwas from Lake Superior. They started to occupy these unoccupied territories left by the Iroquois, first the Manitoulin Island of Georgian Bay, most of the old Huron territory and a lot of southern Ontario.

History is not clear about the attitude of the Iroquois against the new nation. In the late 1600s the Ojibwas with their tribes, the Mississaugas and Chippewas, started to push the Iroquois south across Lake Ontario and completely cleared the area north of Lake Ontario. In 1784 most of Ontario, except for a few military posts, was occupied by the Chippewa nation.

By the time of the American War of Independence they had completely cleared the Iroquois from Ontario. After the cessation of the war the people who fought for the British along with parts of the Iroquois nation looked north for a place to live without fear of persecution. In 1784 Governor

Haldimand purchased 700,000 acres from the Mississaugas for the Six Nations reserve at the Grand Valley and also a reserve of Deseronto. Other early land purchased was by Lord Simcoe, from Niagara to Toronto.

In 1791 the new province of Ontario was formed from Upper and Lower Canada. By the end of 1700s most of the loyal Iroquois had settled on Ontario reserves. By now English, Scottish, and Irish people were immigrating to Ontario in large numbers. The province then started to purchase land from the Mississaugas and Chippewas. By the late 1700s it had purchased eight parcels, and it bought more in 1806 to 1836. Another parcel covering an area north of Belleville to the Ottawa River was bought in 1787–8 (see map, lot 2).

In the early 1800s, many of the Mississaugas and Chippewas had villages throughout Ontario. They decided to form new reserves. Larger villages were broken down and formed into small reserves. The Chippewas of Lake Huron and Simcoe were ready to surrender portions of three bands and split into smaller bands, the Rama, Snake Island, and Beausoleil. Later they settled at Coldwater and moved to Christian Island. As the province had given up the practice of giving presents to the natives, it decided to help them on the land with farm machinery, seeds, and help to build homes. Small groups went on their own. One of these wandering bands was the Mississaugas of the Bay of Quinte, who roamed around Kingston and Gananoque.

Around 1835–36 a large group of Chippewas who had surrendered their land at Georgian Bay came through the Gananoque and Cataraqui Rivers and started a settlement called Chippewa. They built a Roman Catholic church and school at Chaumont in the township of Camden. The area

Chippewas and the church still exist. The Chippewas saved a parcel of land for their own use, but it was never used.

Logging started on the Ottawa River in 1804, affecting the Algonquins and the fur trade. According to historian Lloyd Jones, the Chippewas' land was offered to a wandering group of Algonquins. They refused it, and many left the Ottawa River area. They dispersed, except for one family, who started a farm at Dalhousie Lake. The government gave the Algonquins 37,500 acres for a reserve on Desert River at Maniwaki, where most of the Algonquins from the southern area settled. Other Algonquin reserves later were allotted land farther north of the Ottawa River waterways. The reserve on Desert River at Maniwaki was given to the Algonquins in 1853, and the Golden Lake Reserve was granted to the Algonquins in 1858.

In 1848 during the great potato famine in Ireland, many Irish immigrants settled in the Chippewa area and used the Roman Catholic church and schools. The second generation of young Chippewas moved north to the Wolfe and Desert Lake area.

Church of the Annunciation of the Blessed Virgin Mary, Chippewa (Douglas Anderson). Source: author's personal notes.

At this point the government was trying to settle the northern rocky area of Frontenac. Land could be bought for just the cost of registration. John Antoine and his wife, Whiteduck, both purebred Chippewa, bought 200 acres at Devil Lake. John followed the nature trail from Crow Lake through the water system to Depot Lakes in search of ginseng, which was sold to China. This trail showed signs of a lot of use, as the Iroquois had used it for many years.

John Antoine was hunting in the 1860s in the Sharbot Lake area when he met Francis Sharbot and Currie, a potash man. John Antoine later bought what is now known as Antoine Point in Sharbot Lake. During the 1930s many of the Chippewas moving north would stop at the Antoine home.

Bill Beaver settled on the Mississippi River below Ardoch, his daughter on the Mississauga reserve at Rice Lake. The Nogen family was given trees and land on the Antoine property to build the shanty and stayed the winter making baskets from basswood logs. After the Iroquois left Ontario, the first native settlers in Frontenac County were the Chippewas. At Sharbot Lake the only native was John Antoine, Francis Sharbot, and the St. Pierres, who had left the reserve at Deseronto and were Mohawk.

These three families assimilated with other pioneers and were known as Indians. The tribes they came from were not referred to by them or other people in the community. These pioneers cleared land, rock, and swamp and helped to build the community along with our country.

DONALD M. ANTOINE

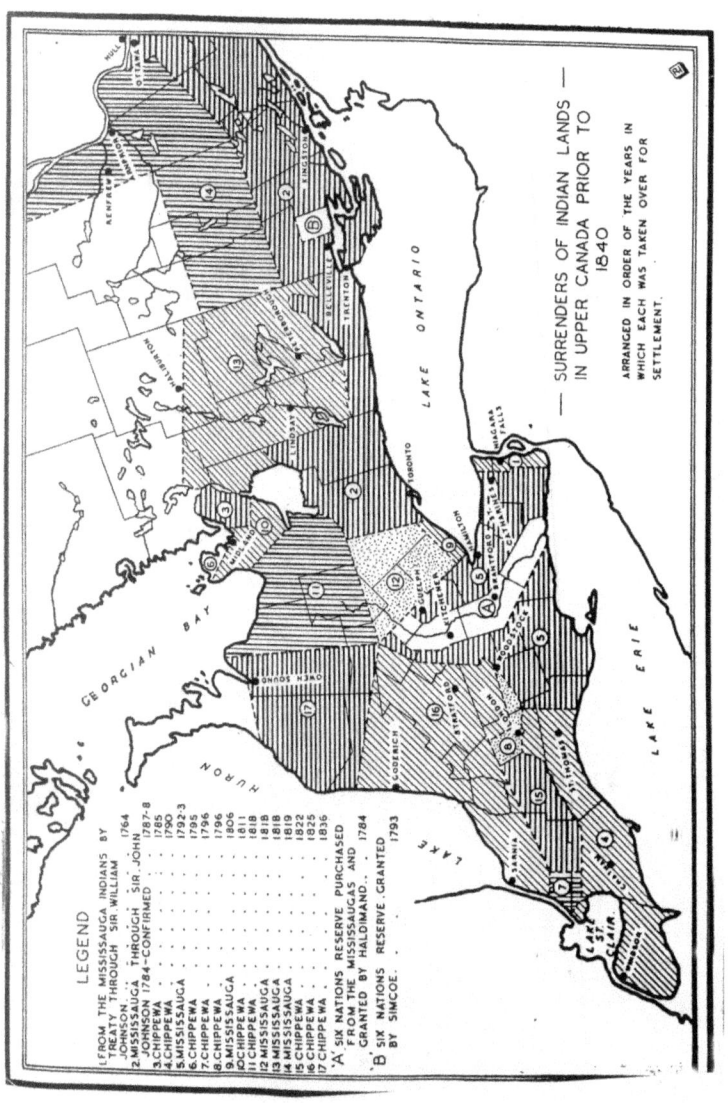

THE SPIRIT OF THE THUNDERBIRD

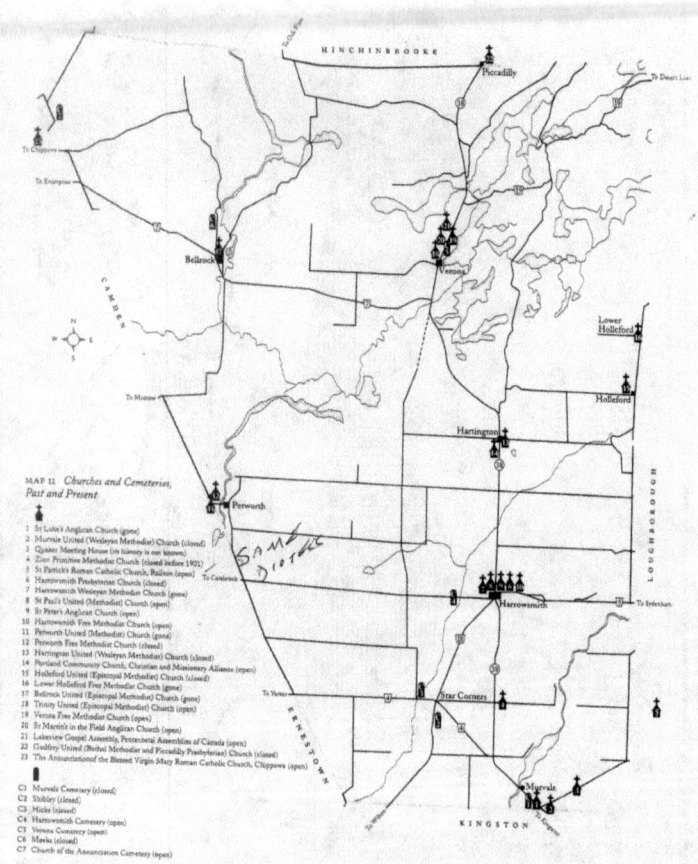

MAP 11 *Churches and Cemeteries, Past and Present*

1. St Luke's Anglican Church (gone)
2. Murvale United (Wesleyan Methodist) Church (closed)
3. Quaker Meeting House (its history is not known)
4. Zion Primitive Methodist Church (closed before 1921)
5. St Patrick's Roman Catholic Church, Railton (open)
6. Harrowsmith Presbyterian Church (closed)
7. Harrowsmith Wesleyan Methodist Church (gone)
8. St Paul's United (Methodist) Church (gone)
9. St Peter's Anglican Church (open)
10. Harrowsmith Free Methodist Church (open)
11. Petworth United (Methodist) Church (gone)
12. Petworth Free Methodist Church (closed)
13. Hartington United (Wesleyan Methodist) Church (closed)
14. Portland Community Church, Christian and Missionary Alliance (open)
15. Holleford United (Episcopal Methodist) Church (closed)
16. Lower Holleford Free Methodist Church (gone)
17. Bellrock United (Episcopal Methodist) Church (gone)
18. Trinity United (Episcopal Methodist) Church (open)
19. Verona Free Methodist Church (open)
20. St Martin's in the Field Anglican Church (open)
21. Lakeview Gospel Assembly, Pentecostal Assemblies of Canada (open)
22. Godfrey United (Bethel Methodist and Piccadilly Presbyterian) Church (closed)
23. The Annunciation of the Blessed Virgin Mary Roman Catholic Church, Chippewa (open)

C1. Murvale Cemetery (closed)
C2. Shibley (closed)
C3. Hicks (closed)
C4. Harrowsmith Cemetery (open)
C5. Verona Cemetery (open)
C6. Marks (closed)
C7. Church of the Annunciation Cemetery (open)

References

Native Peoples of the Canadian Experience, 2nd and 3rd ed.

The Valley of the Iroquois.

The Champlain Papers.

The Department of Native Affairs, Ontario and Quebec.

History of Portland Township.

chapter 2

HISTORY OF THE IROQUOIS NATION

All natives of North America walked across the Bering Strait, went down the Pacific Coast to what is now the Gulf of Mexico, and came north in smaller groups over a period of 2,000 to 3,000 years. We do not know when they arrived in the present area.

Iroquoian refers to the Iroquois' spoken language; *Iroquois* refers to the tribe.

The Iroquoian speakers include the St. Lawrence Iroquois, Huron, Neutrals (Wenro), Petuns (Wyandot), and the Tobacco People. Linguistics studies show some nouns in the Cherokee tribe were similar to the Iroquois'.

According to their own oral history, Iroquois have been on the "Island of the Turtle" (the North American continent) since time immemorial; they still call themselves the "People of the Turtle."

The first Iroquoian people of which there is historical evidence is the St. Lawrence or Laurentian tribe. First documented by Jacques Cartier in 1535, there were longhouse villages at Stadncona (Quebec City) and Hochelaga (Montreal) and seven to ten villages along the St. Lawrence as far west as Richelieu River.

A seigniory on Montreal Island was given to LaSalle in 1667.

Many Jesuit, Récollets, and other monks soon learned after staying in the winter camps, with great tepees holding around twenty-five natives and dogs, that Christianization was not successful. In 1718 the Sulpician Monks were given a seigniory on the Lake of Two Mountains to build a village of churches and schools known as Oka to Christianize the Algonquians. This plan failed because the Algonquians had a migratory and nomadic lifestyle, hunting, fishing, and gathering supplies for the winter months.

There was not a chief. They had many groups, with a headman as their leader, moving many times to different territories. They would stay for a short time in one place set up so they could move in one day, by canoe in the summer and toboggan in the winter. It was common to be away from Oka for many months of the year.

Four reserves had been formed in Lower and Upper Canada during the American War of Independence. Many tribes along the American Atlantic coast had been ordered west of the Mississippi River, and natives were adopted by the Mohawks and sent to Oka.

Oka is an Algonquin name and was accepted and still remains so. The Mohawk name is Kanesatake. In 1720 the Mohawks joined the Algonquins at Oka. They lived in harmony and remained one of the main trading areas for the Algonquins.

The war between the French and Iroquois was settled in 1701. The Mohawks started in agriculture, and many Algonquins learned farming. In the 1820s the government started cutting off money and gave aid to farming.

While the Mohawks were in complete control of Oka, the Sulpician Monks started to sell timber to England to build ships. This caused trouble between the Mohawks and the monks, and by the early 1800s many of the Mohawks had left.

The Gibson Reserve as established at Lake Simcoe and others went west but later returned to Oka.

The federal government bought Oka from the Sulpician Monks in 1815. Twenty years ago a golf course attempted to expand into Mohawk ancestral burial grounds at Oka. During the Mohawk efforts to protect their land a Quebec police officer was shot. Ten years after this fight for land, in 2000, the federal government turned the rights to Oka to the Mohawks after holding these rights for 195 years.

The Iroquois fought among each other intertribal wars for many years. Finally in the 1500s they decided to end the senseless wars and make what was called "The Great Peace." They established the Confederation of Five Nations of the Iroquois People. In the words of the editors of the Smithsonian handbook of the North American Indians it was the most remarkable civil organization in the new world except for Mexico and Peru. These five tribes were the Mohawk, Cayuga, Oneida, Onondaga, and Seneca. Never again would there be war between any of these Iroquois people, and no tribe would be permitted to war against any other people without the sanction of the league.

Iroquois settlements in Canada today are Kahnawake/Caughnawana, Kanesatake, Mohawk/Oka, Lake of Two Mountains, Gibson/Wahta, Akwesasne/St. Regis, Six Nations/Grand River, Tyendinega, and Oneida on the Thames (see maps).

For centuries historians have written of the "political genius" of the Iroquois. They have been called "the Romans of the West."

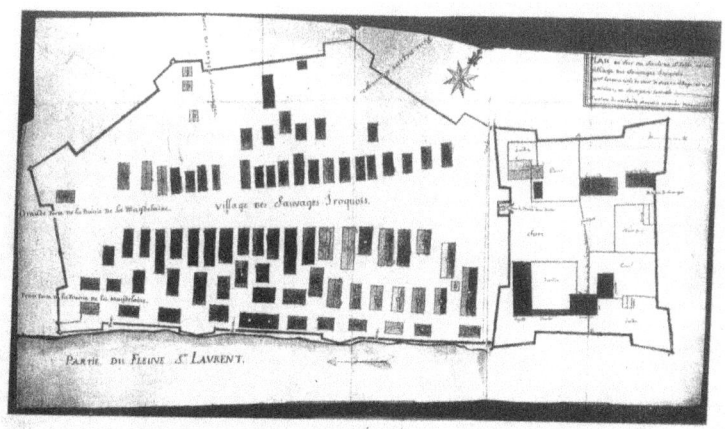

Plan du Fort de Sault de St. Louis Villages des Iroquois (Kahnawake), mid-eighteenth century. (Ayer M.S. Map 2011 in Ayer M.S. 299 Courtesy of the Edward E. Ayer Collection, The Newberry Library, Chicago. Source: Indians of Quebec & the Maritime Provinces, Indian Review.

During the American War of Independence the Iroquois wampum belt was buried, but after the war Brant and Benjamin Franklin reviewed the belt, and when the constitution of the United States was drawn, many of the most crucial clauses were based on the principal of the Confederacy of the Iroquois People.

By the time Champlain arrived in 1603, the St. Lawrence Iroquois had disappeared. Archeology suggests they may have joined local tribes, but none of the local tribes were big enough to absorb 4,000 to 5,000 people. They probably joined the Iroquois south and north of Lake Ontario.

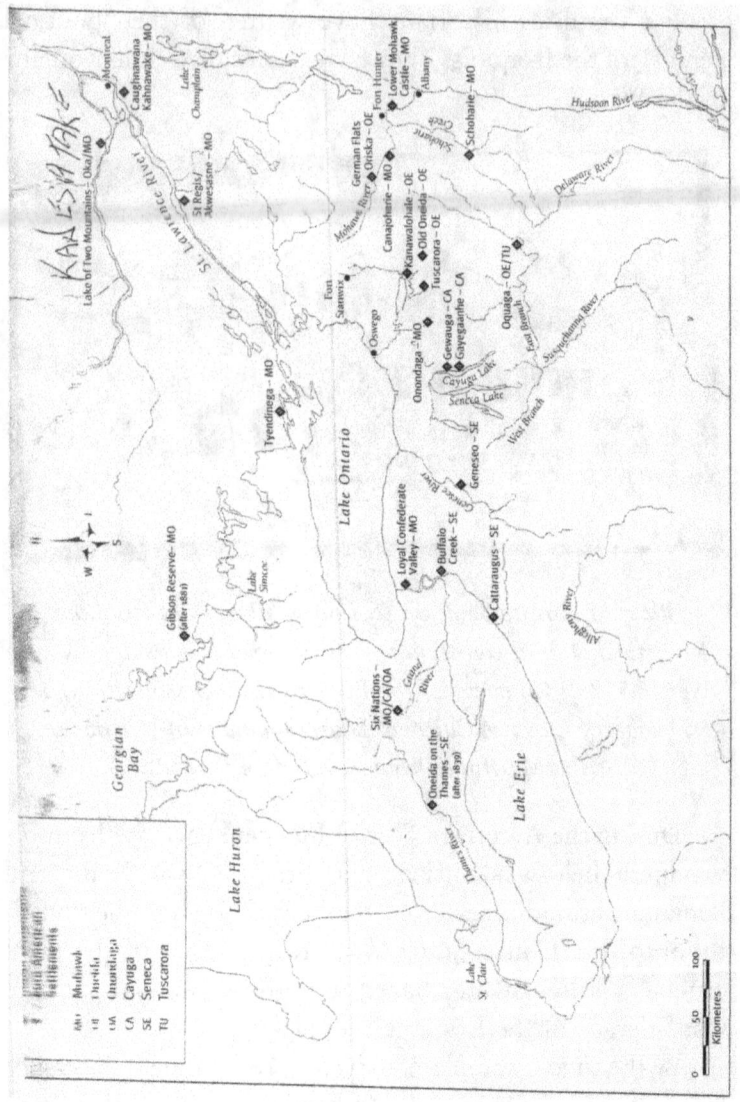

Iroquois Settlements, circa 1784.
Source: Indians of Ontario Review

The Iroquoian speaking people lived in primarily sedentary villages, which they moved every ten to twelve years when nutrients in the soil were exhausted and it was no longer good for the growth of corn, beans, and squash. At moving time they had the "Feast of the Dead." Like the Huron, during the feast for the dead they would disinter the bones to reunite the spirits with their relatives. After the feast they would reinter the bones and place them into a bone pit.

The Iroquois lived in villages surrounded by palisades, which provided a defence against enemies. There were as many as thirty longhouses in the largest villages, ranging from eight to thirty metres in length. Each was capable of sheltering fifteen or twenty families. The houses were shaped like barns, with walls and gabled roofs of cedar or elm bark laid over a framework of poles. At either end there was a doorway and down both sides a row of cubicles, each the home of a family. In summer the residents slept on benches against the walls. For greater warmth in the winter they used sleeping mats spread on the floor near the family fires, which were located along the centre aisle of the house.

chapter 3

THE COLONIZATION OF QUEBEC, 1608–1763

In 1603 Samuel de Champlain arrived in Stadacona and Hochelaga. It took a few years to take an interest in Quebec. When it was decided to colonize New France, many men from France came in. As fur trading was the primarily objective, the fur trading post at Three Rivers was founded in 1634. Settlers were sent out with stores and equipment to trade, and the Marquis de Tracy arrived with 1,000 men and 100 officers. They eventually had 60,000 settlers.

The next group of settlers comprised 2,000 people. At this point the whole of the St. Lawrence River west to the Richelieu was divided up by the seignior system, all with a short waterfront with a great depth. The seignior plots were all given out, and the principal purpose was the growth of farm products to supply the towns and to fight for New France in case of war. These institutions were continually under raid by the Iroquois.

chapter 4

HISTORY OF FRENCH IROQUOIS WAR STARTED BY CHAMPLAIN

No evidence has been found to prove that any white man had visited Lake Champlain prior to the year 1609. In that year Samuel Champlain, "Father of New France," agreed to accompany the Huron, Montagnais, and Algonquin Indians against their powerful enemies to the south, the Iroquois or Five Nations. Near the end of June, Champlain with eleven Frenchmen and his

Samuel de Champlain and Algonquin Indians in battle with the Iroquois. Source: author's personal notes

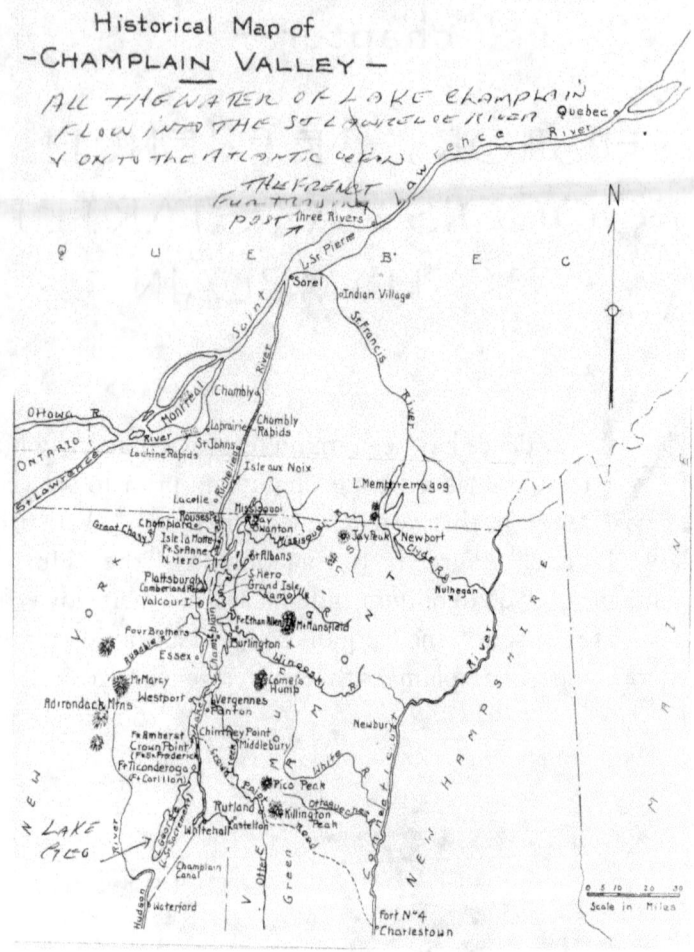

Indian allies started on a war expedition into Iroquois country. Two days were spent at the mouth of the Richelieu. A disagreement arising as to war plans caused some of the Indians to decide to return home. Only two of the Frenchmen in the party volunteered to proceed with their leader. The war party set out in twenty-four canoes, two white men and sixty Indians.

I can only use some salient points from the book of *The Champlain Papers*. Leaving the Richelieu, they entered Lake Champlain on July 4. Beside the great beauty of the Pine Islands many fishing and hunting stories were told by the natives, whose ancestors had fought the same enemies in times long past. They rested in the day and travelled at night. On the third day they were approaching the Iroquois territory.

The story of the battle was told by Champlain:

> When evening came we embarked in our canoes to continue on our way; and as we were going along very quietly with no noise we met the Iroquois at ten o'clock at night at the end of a cape that projected into the lake on the west side. They were coming to war. We both began making loud cries, each getting his arms ready.
>
> We withdrew toward the shore, and the Iroquois went ashore and arranged their canoes in a line and began to cut trees, and they barricaded themselves well. Our own men also passed the whole night within arrow range from the barricade. The whole night war passed in dances and song and endless insults back and forth. Huron spoke the same language as did some of the Algonquin.
>
> As we armed ourselves with light armour, the enemy came out of the barracks, 200 men; at their heads were the chiefs who wore large plumes. As soon as we went ashore we began to run about 200 paces toward the enemy. We divided into two parts, me going into the woods. As I advanced toward them, each looking at the other, I saw them make a move to shoot us. I rested my Arquebuse on my cheek and aimed at the three chiefs and shot. Two chiefs fell to

the ground dead, the other died later from the wounds. Meanwhile arrows did not fail to fly from both sides. As I was loading again one of my companions fired a shot from the woods, which astonished them, and seeing their three dead chiefs took to flight and abandon the fort fleeing deep into the woods. We pursued them and killed more of them. Our savages also killed several and took ten to twelve prisoners. About fifteen of our men were wounded by arrows, but healed soon.

Our people amused themselves by taking great quantities of corn from the enemies, also arms which they left in order to run. And having a good time dancing and singing, we returned home a few hours after with our prisoners.

Where the battle was fought was hard to establish, but the route taken by Lake George necessitated passing by rapids, which means the place was Ticonderoga.

Champlain died in 1635. The new governor, Denonville, continued the battle with many attacks, but the Iroquois kept their battle up against the French settlers.

They planted corn in the mounds, beans between the corn hills, and squash in separate plots. This comprised 80 percent of their diet. The men went on hunting and trading expeditions in the summer, leaving the women at home to tend and harvest the crops. Corn was stored in large bark chests inside the houses and squash in bark-lined pits outside. Many of the varieties of corn and beans in use today were developed by the Indians, and ancient Indian recipes are still used for cooking corn. Every Iroquoian community was surrounded by several hundred acres of cornfields, and the larger villages raised as many as 150,000 bushels of corn in a single season.

When not cultivating the cornfields the women and children gathered acorns, butternuts, chestnuts, and hickory nuts, and also raspberries, blueberries, cranberries, and wild plums. They collected small quantities of sugar maple sap but did not make enough sugar to store away for the winter months.

Cooking utensils consisted of clay cooking pots, paddles for stirring corn and berries, ladles and bowls of bark and wood, bark chests for storage of corn, mortars and pestles for grinding it, and baskets, sleeping mats, and skins. Tools consisted of stone-bladed axes and knives; wooden drills for kindling fires; bone awls for husking corn and punching holes in wood, bark and skin; and bone scrapers for dressing skins. Iroquoian mothers carried their babies in wooden cradles. Ornaments were made of bones, stones, and shells.

Iroquoians traded among themselves and, after 1701, with the Algonquian tribes beyond their borders. Wampum was used in trade. It consisted of beads made from clams or other shells by Indians on the New England coast. White wampum meant prosperity, peace, and goodwill; purple wampum symbolized death, disaster, or war. There were four uses for wampum: personal decoration, currency, records (in the form of strings joined together), and the ratification of treaties (in the form of belts and sashes).

The native canoes of the Iroquoians made from elm bark were rather crude, although some had birchbark canoes purchased from the Algonquians. They generally traveled on foot and in the winter with the aid of snowshoes. They carried burdens in wicker baskets suspended from the forehead by a wide strap. Warriors often carried a long cord of plaited fibre to serve as a pack-strap and for tying captured prisoners.

From childhood the Iroquoians were trained as warriors. The possession of corn enabled them to remain in the field for a longer period and in greater numbers than their enemies, who had to disperse to hunt and fish after a few days. The early weapons were knobbed wooden clubs, sometimes fitted with stone spikes, and the bow and arrow. After the Europeans came, tomahawks were used. Many warriors wore armour of wooden slats and carried wooden shields covered with rawhide, but this equipment was useless after the Indians obtained firearms.

Many festivals occurred throughout the year. Women participated in the public dances and joined the men's games, although they had special games of their own. The game of lacrosse was the most popular athletic recreation, and the whole village took sides against each other. The Iroquoians, who were fond of gambling, bet on their athletic games and on several games of pure chance similar to dice.

The Iroquoians believed in two great spirits, one good, the other evil, each governing a throng of lesser spirits. At the festivals they made public prayers to the good spirits, burning tobacco as a thank-offering. Most men and many women carried charms, supposedly obtained from spirits in dreams, and they trusted religious societies or clubs to keep away the evil spirits. The members of the False Face society placed grotesque masks over their faces, spring and autumn, and invaded all the village houses to banish the demons that brought human disease.

The Iroquoian were fond of singing and used it as a an accompaniment to all their dances. They chanted many prayers and incantations and had war and victory chants, love songs, and lullabies. The love songs were simple melodies played on a six-holed flute. The medicine man had a rattle made of the top shell of a turtle filled with small seeds, which he used to accompany his healing chants. A tambourine provided rhythm for certain ceremonies. Orators had great eloquence and dignified gestures.

The only Iroquoian wood carvings were the False Face masks. Stone and clay pipes were sometimes carved or modelled into human or other forms, and small ornaments were shaped to resemble birds or other objects. Pottery was decorated by incising or impressing. Some decorative embroidery was done with porcupine quills, but beadwork and silk embroidery were post-European developments.

During the American Revolutionary War a large number of the Six Nations Indians fought for the British cause under the leadership of the celebrated Mohawk chief Thayendanegea, or Joseph Brant. Brant had fought on the British side during Pontiacs war in 1763 and had visited England in 1775. He received a captain's commission and distinguished himself in several battles. He was the leader of his people until his death in 1807.

After the Treaty of Paris in 1783 the traditional lands of the Six Nations became United States territory, and many of the Iroquois under Brant wished to move to Canada, where they would still be under the British flag. Governor Haldimand granted to the Six Nations a large block of the most valuable land in Ontario, containing about 675,000 acres, along the Grand River, which flows into Lake Erie. This land was purchased from the aboriginal occupants, the Mississaugas.

While Joseph Brant and the majority of his Indians decided to take up lands on the Grand River, a group of Mohawks under the leadership of John Deserontyon or "John the Mohawk," one of Brant's lieutenants in the Revolutionary War, determined to settle at the Bay of

Quinte on Lake Ontario. These Indians persisted in their determination, although General Haldimand and Joseph Brant both urged them to go to the Grand River with the rest of the Six Nations Indians. The day of their arrival at the Bay of Quinte is celebrated by their descendants each year on Mohawk Sunday, the Sunday nearest May 22, and a cairn marks their landing place.

Prior to 1784, southwestern Ontario, with the exception of a few military posts, was occupied by the Indians. After 1784 a large influx of United Empire Loyalists to Canada led to the creation in 1791 of the new provinces of Upper and Lower Canada, Upper Canada being the older part of the present province of Ontario. Many Americans moved into the new province until by 1812 the population had grown to about 80,000. The settlers developed agriculture, fishing, lumbering, and commerce, pushing the ancient industry of the fur trade into a slow decline and fall and weakening the whole economic basis of the Indian culture.

During the years between 1818 and 1836, several agreements were negotiated with the Indians in order to obtain land for the large numbers of immigrants who were arriving from England, Scotland, and Ireland.

Despite the migration to Manitoulin Island, the northern coasts of Lakes Huron and Superior still remained largely occupied by nomadic bands of Chippewa Indians, who claimed this territory as their hunting grounds. However, by a treaty dated September 7, 1850, the Chippewa Indians surrendered the land on the north shore of Lake Superior, including the islands, from Batchewana Bay to Pigeon River and inland to the height of land, in consideration of an immediate payment of £2,000, an annuity of £500, and the setting aside of permanent reserves.

Also by a treaty of September 9, 1850, the Chippewa Indians surrendered the eastern and northern shores of Lake Huron, including the islands, from Penetanguishene to Batchewana Bay and inland to the height of land, in consideration of the terms similar to the treaty of September 7.

The treaties of 1850 did not prevent the Indians concerned from using the surrendered land. They carried on with their nomadic life much as they had in the past, fishing, hunting, and trapping and trading furs at Hudson's Bay Company posts.

The provincial government attempted to settle the Indians into an agricultural life with good homes, a sufficient and nutritious diet, and provisions made for medical attendance. Annual grants for seed, grain, and implements

A 1786 painting, **Joseph Brant, Mohawk Indian,** *by Gilbert Stuart, who was known for his portraits of men such as George Washington. Notice Brant's silver gorget given to him by his British allies, and the trade silver brooches worn by his very Iroquoian headpiece and European-style collar. Brooches like these and, later, Iroquois-made brooches, had symbols of clans and European church and social groups, such as the masons.*
Source: Ontario School Book History

were given to Indian farmers, and Indian funds were built up from the sales of their lands and timber.

*Left: Four members of a Mohawk delegation were painted by John Verelst in portraits commissioned by Queen Anne during their diplomatic visit in 1710. In one painting, Brant (**Sa Ga Yeath Qua Pieth Tow**), the grandfather of Joseph Brant, wears a scarlet cloak, white cloth shirt, quill-decorated black-dyed moccasins, a powder horn and a burden strap belt. He has a series of blue tattoos over his face and body. The bear in the background indicates Brant's clan. Source: Ontario School Book History*

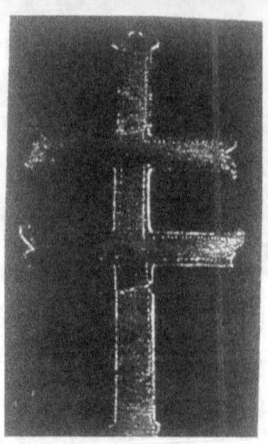

Above: An 18th-century trade silver cross, probably brought by French catholic brothers from France and given to Mohawks in Canada. Source: author's personal notes.

DONALD M. ANTOINE

*A painting, **The Iroquois Tree of Peace**, by Oren Lyons (Onondaga), c. 1970. The Great Law of Peace was proclaimed by **Deganawida**, the Peacemaker. The law established the Iroquois confederacy and set out the principles by which the five nations were to co-operate and live. The Law and the religious authority behind it are symbolized by the white pine growing in the earth on the Grandmother Turtle's back. Animals that represent most of the maternal family clans are grouped around the tree. The clans shown here are Heron, Eagle, Eel, Beaver, Wolf, Bear, Turtle, Snipe, Hawk and Deer. With its four white roots of peace extending north, south, east and west, the pine draws the people together at its base. Source: The Encyclopaedia of the First Peoples of North America*

THE SPIRIT OF THE THUNDERBIRD

This 19th-century wooden Mohawk cradleboard, with an elaborately carved back and simple head piece and footrest, is from the St. Regis area, on the border between Canada and the United States. The baby was bound to the board by a cover (missing) and a tumpline or burden strap.
Source: author's personal notes.

References

Native People: The Canadian Experience, 2nd and 3rd editions.

Champlain Letters.

The Valley of the Six Nations.

History by Indian Affairs, Ontario.

History by Indian Affairs, Quebec.

The Champlain Papers.

Green, Rayna. *The Encyclopaedia of the First Peoples of North America.* Toronto: Groundwood Books, 1999.

chapter 5

THE HURON NATION

The Hurons lived along the shores of Georgian Bay. They had thirty longhouse villages with approximately one thousand people in each. Each village had a chief who would meet once a year. They were further divided into five tribal groupings. The long Indian names had no translation to English. At these meetings they would renew their alliances and review the laws of the wampum.

The Hurons spoke the Iroquois' language. However, they were bitter enemies, and during the summer months their war parties raided each other's lands constantly.

Like the Iroquois the Hurons planted great fields of corn, squash, and beans. These vegetables would be traded with the Algonquians for wild rice and hides when they were on their way to the French fur trading post at Three Rivers.

The Hurons moved their villages every ten to twelve years when the soil became too poor to grow crops. At moving time, like the Iroquois, the Hurons would hold the "Feast of the Dead." During the feast they would disinter the dead to unite the spirits of their relatives; after the feast they would reinter the remains in a bone pit.

The other Iroquois-speaking natives were the Neutrals, Peténs, and Wenros. They were related to the Hurons. Their population was about 28,000, living east of the Hurons in twenty-eight to forty villages. These tribes were decimated in 1647 by the Iroquois, prior to the Battle of Total Elimination of the Hurons a year later in 1648.

The Iroquois lost many lives from the attack of the Hurons at Long Sault Rapids. The French continually attacked their villages along the north shores of Lake Ontario, particularly the large Seneca village Teiaiagon at the mouth of the Humber River, which was destroyed in 1673. The French attacked with one hundred canoes and burned the village and large stocks of corn. Some historians think that the Seneca burned the village themselves and fled as the Iroquois strength weakened.

Father Jean De Brebeuf (Jesuit, 1593-1649)

Father Jean de Brebeuf was assigned to Christianizing the Hurons along the shores of Georgian Bay. The Hurons came with their canoes to take him up the Ottawa River, the Mattawa River to Lake Nippissing, and down the French River to Georgian Bay. To control the Ottawa River, the Algonquians had gathered on Allumette Island and were charging a toll for use of the river.

Jean de Brebeuf had many supplies, such as awls, pins, needles, fishhooks, jackknives, and mirrors. He sent back notes to the other Jesuits to follow carefully the habits and ways of the Hurons. A book written about Jean de Brebeuf was called *The Saint Among the Hurons*.

By 1648, the Jesuits had built eleven or twelve mission stations in the country of the Hurons. Ste. Marie, near present day Midland, was the chief mission. Its buildings were large and well fortified. The missionaries planted corn, squash, and beans. They lived very plainly and were able to supply food to the Indians in times of famine and to entertain them on feast days. More and more Indians were being baptized.

Then the Iroquois struck.

In the summer of 1648 an Iroquois war party fell upon St. Joseph, an Indian village of two thousand people. Missionary Father Daniel was slaughtered and many Indian woman, men, and children with him. The following spring the Iroquois destroyed the villages of St. Ignace and St. Louis and tortured to death two priests, Jean de Brebeuf and Gabriel Lalemant. Father de Brebeuf fought long and hard for his family, the Hurons; he showed no sign of pain. The Iroquois ate his heart to give them some of his strength and courage. The Jesuits had thirty-one monks in this area; seven were killed by the Iroquois.

One after another the Huron villages were attacked, until the only mission that remained was Ste. Marie. At last the Jesuit fathers decided that it was not safe to stay. They burned the mission and took refuge on a small island in Georgian Bay. Here thousands of frightened Hurons came to escape their enemies. There was not enough food on the island for so many people; numbers of them starved, and others went back to the mainland, where the Iroquois fell on them again.

In the end, a few Hurons returned with the Black Robes to Quebec. A handful of Indians whose forefathers fled from Huronia so long ago can still be found in nearby Lorette.

(After Edward Chalfield) Nicholas Vincent Isawanhonhi, a Huron chief, holding a wampum belt. Courtesy of the National Archives of Canada, C38948. Source: author's personal notes

Fort Ste. Marie. Source: author's personal notes

The Battle of Mazinaw Rock

A group of Hurons were fishing on Buckshot Lake when a scout advised them that a war party of Iroquois had discovered them and was on their trail. The Hurons left an easy trail up to the Mazinaw Rock. They hid at the top and let the Iroquois come near the top and met them with a hail of arrows. Many were killed, and many jumped off the rock. This probably was the only victory the Hurons won. The Algonquin took over the area after the Huron had gone.

Mazinaw Rock. Source: author's personal notes

References

Native Peoples of the Canadian Experience, 2nd and 3rd ed.

The Valley of the Iroquois.

The Champlain Papers.

The Department of Native Affairs, Ontario and Quebec.

History of Portland Township.

Material for Tecumseh and Pontiac came from the *Ontario History Book* and a new book on the War of 1812, *Don't Give Up the Ship.*

chapter 6

ALGONQUIAN NORTH WOODLAND NATION

Northern Algonquians have long adapted with success not only to cold, but also to unpredictable and extreme climate conditions. A late spring, for instance, would mean late breakup of lakes and rivers for travel and late arrival of migrating geese and other birds important as food. Less snow cover meant less shelter and lower survival rates for some basic food sources, such as partridge, hare, and other ground-dwelling animals. A dry stream would affect their summer operations.

The Algonquians inhabited the uplands of eastern Canada, a rugged forested region ill-suited to agriculture but teeming with game and with numerous lakes and rivers abounding in fish. Hunting and fishing thus became the principle sources of their food supply. Food shortages often occurred in winter, sometimes causing whole families to die of starvation.

All tribes east of the Cree at James Bay were known as the Northeast Subarctic Natives. The Algonquians were known as the Northeastern Woodland Culture.

Rice was a big trading product, being gathered for many years by the Algonquians in far away lakes and streams, and at one time they went as far as Lake Winnipeg, returning to the lower Ottawa River to trade.

They abandoned this distant area and returned to the Ottawa River and its hundreds of miles of tributaries and great forests. In historic years the fur trade would cause the Cree to expand further south east from James Bay, and the Ojibwa from Lake Superior would expand northeast.

These same natives came to Three Rivers to sell their fur at trading posts. The Algonquians' main trading partners were the Hurons, the Ottawas from Manitoulin Island, the Petuns, and the Tobacco tribes. They were all southwest of Georgian Bay. Corn, beans, squash, and tobacco were the trading products for wild rice.

Years later the Mohawks started to trade here as the war between the French and the Iroquois was settled in 1701. When the European explorers entered the region in the sixteenth century, native people were thriving. Dire effects followed contact with the strangers. Smallpox and other contagious illnesses for which the natives had no immunity cut back the population drastically.

The favourite food was the flesh of the moose, followed by caribou and deer. Rabbits and all varieties of fish were also eaten. They gathered many wild berries and a few edible roots. The Algonquians were skilful at hunting, using snares and traps with as great facility as the bow and arrow. They trapped beaver and bear and snared rabbits and white-tailed deer. For fishing they used bone hooks on their lines, wooden spears with bone points, nets made of nettle fibre, and wicker traps. In autumn they fished at night by the light of birchbark or resinous pine torches in the bows of their canoes, which lured the fish within reach of their spears.

Clothing consisted of shirts, leggings, and moccasins of moose or caribou skin, often beautifully decorated with porcupine quills or moose hair embroidery. The shirts worn by the women reached the ankles, but the shirts of the men reached only to the thighs, and they also wore a breechcloth. Mittens and fur caps were worn in winter. A fur robe served as a sleeping blanket and wrap. Robes and children's shirts were sometimes woven from strands of rabbit fur.

Algonquians lived only a few days in one place, compelled as they were to hunt and fish. As a result they developed a portable dwelling that could be tied on a toboggan or loaded into a canoe. This was the wigwam, a tent usually of birchbark, or in the north of caribou hide, stretched over a conical framework of poles with an opening in the top to let out smoke. Some wigwams were dome-shaped.

Possessions of the Algonquians were limited to what they could carry with them. Rush mats covered the floors. Birchbark baskets and trays, wooden spoons, and fibre bags were household utensils. There were stone-bladed knives for skinning game or stripping bark. Women used bone scrapers for dressing hides and bone awls for punching skin or bark.

The Algonquians invented snowshoes and toboggans and made excellent canoes from birchbark. Women and children did the work of transport as the men had to be free to hunt and fish. In the summer most of the travel was by water in canoes.

Each Algonquian tribe consisted of small bands, each inhabiting a hunting territory. There was no permanent chief, but the most experienced man according to the type of activity engaged in at the time was the leader. Occasionally several bands would unite to celebrate some festival or to enjoy one another's society. Their only enemies were the Five Nations south of the St. Lawrence, and their weapons and armour were the same as those described for the Iroquois.

Mothers carried their babies on their backs, strapped in a wooden cradle or a bag lined with moss. As soon as a young man could support a wife he married, but he had to live with the bride's parents for a year and give them everything he obtained in his hunting. Gambling games were enjoyed by all. They had a number of herbal remedies in case of sickness, one of which was the application of balsam gum to wounds. Another favourite cure was the sweat lodge, a domed tent filled with steam.

The Algonquians believed in a Great Spirit who was too remote to be very interested in human affairs, so they evoked aid from lesser deities like the spirits of nature, the sun, the points of the compass, Mother Earth, and the spirits of birds and animals. Every boy and many girls endured a rigid fast so that a supernatural being might appear in a dream and grant protection. Every hunter carried a charm symbolizing his vision and assuring him of supernatural aid.

Hunters sometimes decorated small fragments of the hides of the animals they killed for food in order to appease their souls. The only Algonquian religious organization was the Grand Medicine Society of the Ojibwa Indians. Community medicine men were members of the society. The members used incantations, charms, and herbs to cause or cure diseases and each summer held secret rites inside a large enclosure of poles and brush.

The Fur Trade

The coming of the fur trade resulted in specialized trapping and trading, with less reliance on traditional substances practice. More time was needed for hunting furs so less time was given to harvesting wild rice and other foods. The traders introduced iron tools, guns, kettles, knives, awls, and axes into the native economy and in exchange received the hides of lynx, foxes, otters, martens, muskrats, and principally beavers. Beaver hats were worn as a mark of prestige in Europe during this period and were much in demand. Intensive trapping led to a scarcity of game in certain sections and to movements of the population for purposes of trade and hunting. The French fur trading post was started at Three Rivers in 1634.

For many years the Algonquians held a gathering on the lower Ottawa River to celebrate "The Survival of the Winter." One year about fifteen hundred natives attended. There would be many games, lacrosse, a game similar to dice for gamblers, and storytelling. They were not great stories with bows and arrows but of mythical magnitude of imaginary creatures in the woods, water, and under leaves. These stories were proclaimed by many native tribes.

After their furs had been traded at Three Rivers, trading would begin at the party. One year the Algonquian had tapped four hundred maple trees and sold maple sugar. The Huron brought a cake of fifty pounds. The Huron, Ottawa, Neutrals, and Tobacco people, with groups and poor hunting, would trade with the Algonquians. There would also be demonstrations of canoe, snowshoes, and basket making. They were made by special tradeswomen.

Algonquian Birchbark Canoes

The territory of their tribes went hundreds of miles up the Ottawa River with hundreds of water tributaries laden with great forests with huge birch trees. When debarked, a piece of birchbark would cover gunwale to gunwale of the canoe, while tribes living in lesser forest areas would strip pieces of birchbark and glue them together. The Iroquois had to use elm bark. The canoe museum in Peterborough has other canoes made of pieces of birchbark.

The Algonquians traded these canoes with other tribes, but not with the Iroquois, until the end of the French Indian war in 1701. The Algonquians also made the great canoes used by the couriers de bois to bring the western fur down from Duluth on Lake Superior. They were very rugged and could be easily patched with pine tar. The canoes were loaded with furs and had six to eight paddles.

The women made the snowshoes and could make a set in one hour. They made special ones for running in the deep snow to chase moose until they tired out, and then they speared them.

In southern Quebec, increasing settlement brought about a slow decline of the fur trade and weakened the traditional Indian economy. At that same time, however, the Indians in the northern areas experienced little change and continued relatively undisturbed in their pursuits of fishing, hunting and trapping.

On August 30, 1851, legislation authorized the setting apart of reserves for the use of certain Indian bands in Quebec. Reserves were set aside in 1854 for the Algonquians and the Tetes de Boules of the St. Maurice River and the Latuques, who lived wholly by hunting and fishing.

The provincial government attempted to settle the Indians into an agricultural life with good homes, a sufficient and nutritious diet, and provisions made for medical attendance. Annual grants for seed, grain, and implements were given to Indian farmers, and Indian funds were built up from the sales of their lands and timber. Also, by a treaty of September 9, 1850, the Chippewa Indians surrendered the eastern and northern shores of Lake Huron, including the Manitoulin Islands, from Penetanguishene to Batchewana Bay, in consideration of terms similar to the treaty of September 7. Although the Algonquians were offered government assistance to move to Manitoulin Island, the settled Indians, in general, did not accept the offer. During the period of 1830 to 1866 the fur and rice trading died off.

In 1853 the government of Upper Canada gave the Algonquians 37,500 acres of land on the Desert River near Maniwaki. The Algonquian left Oka for this new area, but there were a few who had been Christianized, and they joined the Mohawks. In 1829 the government started cutting off money and giving aid to farming.

The Nippissing Algonquian are mentioned often in history, and little is actually recorded about them, yet there are many Algonquians living in the areas west of Mattawa west and north of North Bay. Besides the two reserves mentioned some other smaller reserves were established further north on the Ottawa River. Mattawa was one, and the Golden Lake reserve was established in 1858. The woodland Algonquian people had no experience with agriculture. A change in the way of life for the Algonquian began in 1804 when logging started on the Ottawa River. By 1830, the fur trading had died off, as did trade for wild rice. Many Algonquian began moving about in search for a place to live.

A group of regular size came to Bedford Township, where they were offered land that the Chippewa did not use, but they showed no interest. They suddenly disappeared, except for one family that settled at Lake Delhousie.

THE SPIRIT OF THE THUNDERBIRD

With the opening of Desert Lake Reserve many groups throughout the south took refuge in Desert Lake.

Algonquin snow shoes. Ojibwa, Cree and Inuit made different kinds of snowshoes to suit the many kinds of snow conditions. Source: author's personal notes

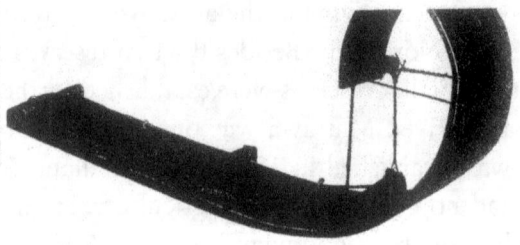

The Algonquin toboggan. Source: author's personal notes

chapter 7

THE CHIPPEWAS AND MISSISSAUGAS OF GREAT LAKE SUPERIOR

The Chippewas and Mississaugas of Great Lake Superior started to move into the uninhabited Georgian Bay area in the late 1600s, and by 1784 they occupied most of Ontario.

The Chippewas and Mississaugas of the Ojibwa tribe moved onto the shores of Georgian Bay and into the Lake Simcoe area. They also occupied the Thames River area and areas of the displaced Neutrals.

The depopulated territories of the Huron, Tobacco, and Neutral nations remained unoccupied for many years. After the Iroquois threat had lessened, Chippewa (Ojibwa) tribes migrated from their hunting ground around Lake Superior to the shores of Huron and Simcoe Lakes. Chippewas also moved into the Thames valley. The Mississauga Ojibwas moved from their hunting grounds on the Upper Lakes to the former territory of the displaced Neutrals.

Much is owed to the early missionaries for the exploration of the wilderness and for the interesting and valuable *Jesuit Relations*, wherein is recorded a detailed description of the country through which the Jesuits travelled and the customs of the native peoples they encountered.

The missionaries learned how to live among the Indians, in their crowded, smoky dwellings, and ate their rough food. They travelled in the Indian manner, by canoe or trail; they wrote reports describing their journeys and made maps of the routes.

The main source of our early written information comes from the Jesuits' and the Recollects' reports. These reports found in monasteries and churches are still used today by historians. The department of Indian Affairs use them in their historical reviews.

chapter 8

PONTIAC: WAR CHIEF OF THE OTTAWAS

The Ottawa tribe fled Manitoulin Isle to Green Bay, now Michigan, to avoid being massacred by the Iroquois in 1649. They grew to a very large nation by the late 1700s.

The French also followed in large numbers, forming trading posts, Jesuit missions and schools, and building Fort Detroit.

About four years after Wolfe captured Quebec, a strange meeting took place on the banks of a river not far from Fort Detroit. Almost five hundred Indian warriors had gathered for the great council of the Confederacy of the Three Fires, which was the name given to three of the tribes who lived between Lake Michigan and Lake Huron. Several other tribes had also been called to the meeting.

At last Pontiac, chief of the Ottawas, arose and walked into the midst of the council. On his head waved his war feathers, and his face and body were painted ready for battle. All the Indians now turned to listen to Pontiac, the cleverest of the chieftains and the most treacherous in war.

"Why," Pontiac demanded, "does the English king send his redcoats into our country to take over the forts where we have always traded with our good friends the French? Why does he not give us presents, as he did the French in years gone by? The French came into our country to trade with us; the English now come to cut down our forests, plant crops, and drive the Indians away forever. Today New France is held by the English, and it is our turn to be destroyed. We must strike now at these English forts in our midst! We must drive out and make war on these dogs clothed in red that will do us nothing but harm!"

Then Pontiac told his listeners of his plans to capture the English forts and to kill the English troops. At this time there were not more then a few hundred British soldiers west of Montreal.

Against them, Pontiac hoped to throw almost fifty thousand Indian warriors. It is not surprising, therefore, that his plan almost succeeded. It is known in Canadian history as the Conspiracy of Pontiac.

Fort Detroit, which was nearby, was the first of the English forts to be attacked by the Indians. Although it never did fall into their hands, the story of how the Indians tried to take it is very interesting because it shows the trickery that Pontiac used in making war. However, things were not going well at the other English forts about the Upper Lakes. One by one, they were attacked by the Indians and destroyed. The soldiers in them were either killed or taken prisoner. Many of them were tortured.

By the end of June, there was not an English soldier left west of Lake Erie, except in Fort Detroit. Fortunately, however, this outpost was able to hold off the Indians all through the summer of 1763, and Pontiac at last gave up his attack. In the meantime, the English had been able to send more troops into the Indian country, and finally peace was made.

A while later Pontiac met the English in a peace council at Oswego, on the southern shore of Lake Ontario. A short time later he met the same fate that he had dealt so many white men. One evening, as he was walking through the woods, another Indian stole after him and struck him down with a tomahawk. So died the war chief of the Ottawas, probably the cleverest and at the same time the most treacherous Indian leader in Canadian history.

References

The Canadian History Book.

chapter 9

THE STORY OF A SHAWNEE CHIEF: TECUMSEH

In the wilds to the south and west of Lake Erie dwelt a tribe of Indians known as the Shawnees. As new settlers from the young United States of America began to clear this part of the country, the Shawnees and their neighbouring tribes grew fearful lest they should be driven from their homes.

The Shawnees had a great chief named Tecumseh. Tecumseh knew that his people might have to fight, but he also knew that they could not fight the United States alone. However, Tecumseh had heard that there was going to be trouble between the Americans and the British to the north, and this gave him an idea. He travelled to Upper Canada to see the British leaders. He told them that he and many thousands of Indian warriors were ready to fight on the side of Canada against the United States.

When war broke out between Great Britain and the United States, Tecumseh and his warriors made their camp on an island in the Detroit River. The British were very much worried about American forces in Fort Detroit, which lay near by. They knew that if the Americans crossed the Detroit River and entered the western part of Upper

Canada, they would have to rush more troops from Niagara to hold the invaders back. This they did not want to do, because there were not enough British troops even to guard the Niagara. Canada was in very great danger in 1812, because there were more than sixteen times as many colonists in the United States as there were on our side of the border.

As soon as fighting broke out at Detroit, Tecumseh led his warriors into battle against the Americans, as he had promised. In one fight alone, Tecumseh and seventy of his followers were able to trap a force of two hundred American soldiers on horseback.

Tecumseh planned this attack so well that over half the Americans were killed, while only one of his warriors lost his life.

General Brock now returned to Lake Ontario, where the Americans were getting ready to attack across the Niagara River. But Tecumseh's work was not finished, and he stayed on. The next year the Americans sent fresh troops to recapture Detroit, and the new British leader there was forced to retreat. Tecumseh did not like the idea of retreating, but he ordered his warriors to fall back with the British, fighting as they went.

At last, Tecumseh persuaded the British general to stop retreating and meet the Americans who were following them. As soon as the British leader agreed to do so, Tecumseh called his Indians together for a council meeting.

"Brother warriors," he cried, "we are now about to enter a battle from which I shall never come out. My body will remain in the field of battle."

Tecumseh was right. The British soldiers were tired and hungry before the fight began, and the Americans soon broke through their lines. Only a handful escaped altogether. In the height of the battle, Tecumseh caught sight of the American leader. Shouting his war cry and waving his tomahawk above his head, he rushed through his warriors to strike him down. But the American leader saw him coming, aimed his pistol at the Indian chief, and shot Tecumseh through the heart. Tecumseh had fought in several engagements but was killed at Chatham on the Thames River, October 5, 1813.

That night, after the fighting was over, some of the Indian warriors who had fought with the British returned to the battlefield. Almost at the edge of the American camp they found the body of their fallen leader, and they carried it away.

The Treaty of Ghent ended the war in 1814.

There is no monument today over the grave of this great Indian chief. Only the Indians knew where they buried their dead leader, and they kept their secret well.

November 7, 1811, Gov. William Henry Harrison took one thousand regular troops and destroyed "The Prophet's" town. Tecumseh's brother was known as "The Prophet." The battle took place at Tippecanoe, near present day Lafayette, Indiana.

DONALD M. ANTOINE

*Tecumseh (1768?-1813) was the great Shawnee leader who sought to mold North American Indians into a confederation. His pan-Indian movement did not survive his death at the Battle of the Thames in 1813. There is no surviving portrait of Tecumseh, but this sketch, by Benson J. Lossing, was drawn from a pencil sketch, now lost, made by Pierre le Dru around 1808. (Lossing, **Pictorial Field-Book of the War of 1812.**) Source: Ontario School History Book*

THE SPIRIT OF THE THUNDERBIRD

*Tenskwatawa, better known as the Prophet (1768-1837), was Tecumseh's brother and the founder of a pan-Indian religious movement that Tecumseh transformed into a political and military alliance. The Prophet suffered a blow from the Indian defeat at Tippecanoe but still retained significant influence. (Lossing, **Pictorial Field-Book of the War of 1812.**)*
Source: Ontario School History Book

References

The Canadian History Book.

chapter 10

MAJOR GENERAL SIR ISAAC BROCK

General Brock had prepared Upper Canada against invasion as well as he could, since war had been feared for several years. Volunteer soldiers had been trained carefully and, along with the British regulars, were stationed at posts along the border. Even though Canadians were encouraged by Brock's capture of Detroit during the early days of the war, they knew that the danger of invasion was still great. The greatest danger now lay along the Niagara River, between Lake Erie and Lake Ontario, where the Americans had gathered about seven thousand troops.

When General Brock left Tecumseh at Detroit, he hurried to the Niagara River frontier. Here he found fewer than fifteen hundred men to guard the Canadian shore against an attack by the Americans across the river. If the Americans gained a foothold on the Canadian bank, they might overrun the Niagara Peninsula and reach Dundas Road—the main highway joining York, the capital, with the western part of the province. Upper Canada would then be cut in two.

General Brock was at Fort George, at the mouth of the Niagara, on the night of October 12. Shortly after midnight, the Americans began to cross the river at Queenston. At first it was not clear whether this was to be their main attack or only a feint to draw the main British force away from Fort George. Leaving his second-in-command, General Sheaffe, a brave and able office, with orders to follow with the troops from Fort George if the American main attack turned out to be at Queenston, Brock rode along the river to see for himself what was happening. On the way he met a messenger with news that a great many of the enemy had crossed the river and more and more were coming over. On learning this Brock sent the messenger to Fort George with orders to General Sheaffe to hurry the soldiers along as quickly as possible.

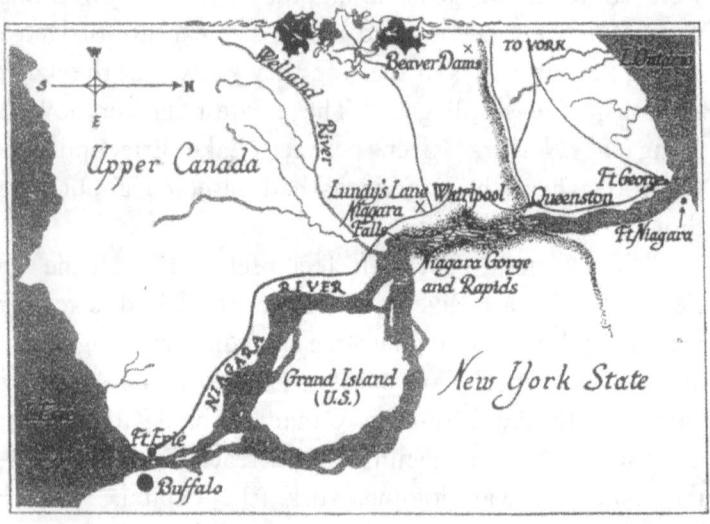

The Niagara Frontier. Source: author's personal notes

The village of Queenston lies at the foot of Queenston Heights, a steep cliff some 350 feet high rising from the edge of the Niagara River. A British gun had been placed on the top of the Heights, but the Americans climbed a steep and narrow path that brought them up behind the British gunners, who then had to beat a hasty retreat. Brock rallied his men for a charge and, with drawn sword, led them up the steep hill. The ranks of the Americans broke, and success seemed sure, when Brock himself was struck down by a shot and almost instantly killed. Dismayed, the British and Canadian lines faltered and then retreated to the foot of the hill, carrying their dead leader with them and leaving the Americans in control of the Heights.

The Americans did not enjoy their success for long. General Sheaffe, who now took command, rallied his men and by a brilliant and daring movement struck inland with his forces. Led by Indian guides, he made a surprise attack on the flank of the Americans, who then had to fight with their backs to the river. Although they still greatly outnumbered the British and Canadians, about fifteen hundred of them having already crossed the river, they were soon overpowered.

The Americans on the Heights now tried desperately to escape. Some managed to row back across the river; others tried to swim, but many were drowned. Some even threw themselves over the cliff. Most of them, however, surrendered to the British and Canadians.

It was a costly victory, for the British had lost a great leader and a great soldier in General Brock. A lofty monument in his honour now stands on the Heights on which he fell. It reminds us how courage, patriotism, and brilliant military skill once more saved Canada from a larger and more powerful invading army.

The First Major Battle: Queenston Heights

As discussed, on October 13, 1812, the United States invaded Canada across the Niagara River. The objective was modest: the establishment of a lodgement on the Canadian side of the river, essentially as a diversion in favour of what was supposed to be the main attack on Montreal. An assault force of U.S. regulars and New York militia that ultimately was commanded by Winfield Scott secured a position on Queenston Heights and waited for additional militia to cross the river to reinforce them. But the militiamen stayed put, citing their constitutional right to refuse to serve on foreign soil. As a result, a combined force of British regulars,

American troops were able to cross the Niagara River and scale the formidable bluffs at Queenston Heights but could not overcome the refusal of New York militia to reinforce them. The result was a decisive Anglo-Indian victory in the first major battle of the war. (Lossing, **Pictorial Field-Book of the War of 1812**). Source: *author's personal notes*

This picture, inaccurate in many details, depicts Major General Issac Brock's death in the romantic manner of battlefield deaths popularized by artist Benjamin West in the eighteenth century. (Painting by John D. Kelly. Library and Archives Canada.)
Source: author's personal notes

Canadian militia, and Indians overwhelmed the American army and compelled it to surrender. Although Major General Isaac Brock was killed in a hastily organized counterattack, the British victory at Queenston Heights was decisive in this theatre, for it effectively ended American operations on the Niagara front in 1812.

Queenston Heights is sometimes portrayed as the first battle of the war, but by this time there had already been significant campaigning in the west. In addition, it was not even the first battle on the Niagara frontier, since four days before a fierce musket and artillery duel had erupted on the Niagara River when an American force surprised the British and seized the brigs *Detroit* and *Caledonia*. The battle of Queenston Heights is better remembered as the first major land battle of the war in which there were significant casualties on both sides and as the decisive battle on the Niagara front in 1812.

Why Did America Militia Refuse to Fight?

Although the New York militia claimed that they could not be forced to serve on foreign soil, this claim should be taken with a grain of salt. In the spring of 1812, Congress had publicly debated whether militia could serve beyond American borders, and no doubt some New York militia learned their rights from this debate, which was widely reported in the press. However, these men were mostly Republicans, who probably knew what was expected of them when they were marched north in the summer of 1812.

Major General Issac Brock (1769-1812) won a dramatic victory at Detroit before being killed in the Battle of Queenston Heights in 1812. Today, Canadians revere him as a great hero. (Portrait by unknown artist. Library and Archives Canada.)
Source: *author's personal notes*

*In this sketch of Queenston Heights, Major General Brock's cenotaph (erroneously placed in 1860) appears in the foreground and the second monument honoring the fallen hero is in the background. (Lossing, **Pictorial Field-Book of the War of 1812**). Source: author's personal notes*

It seems more likely that these "sunshine patriots" were unnerved by the sound of gunfire and the war cries that came from across the river and by the sight of the dead and wounded who were ferried back into American territory. "The commencement of this battle," said an observer, "and a considerable number of dead and mangled bodies which were brought to our shore in the return boats, caused a depression of mind on this side which could not be effaced...None of the militia could be got to cross, and many were constantly deserting."

The sight of additional British regulars marching up from Fort George to reinforce their comrades at Queenston only served to increase the determination of American militia to stay put.

Had the American attack met with little resistance, most of the militia probably would have crossed the river. A failure of nerve, not constitutional scruples, probably best explains why so many citizen soldiers chose to sit out this battle.

Did Brock Have a Fiancée?

Legend has it that Brock said goodbye to his fiancée, Sophie Shaw, on the way to meet his destiny at Queenston Heights. Although he once had an interest in a woman in Britain, there is no evidence that he was ever engaged to be married or that he had any romantic ties in Canada.

The Legend of Brock's Horse

The iconography of Queenston Heights often depicts Brock on a horse named Alfred. There is even a small bronze statue of Alfred encased in a glass box at Queenston. The inscription says that Brock and later his aide, Lieutenant Colonel John Macdonell, rode this horse into battle at Queenston Heights and that Alfred (along with both riders) was killed that day. The horse's role in the battle has even been commemorated in a pamphlet.

Although Brock rode a horse from Fort George to Queenston Heights, the notion that it was Alfred did not appear in print until 1859. When Governor General Sir James Craig departed from Quebec for Britain in June 1811, he left Brock a horse named Alfred, but it is unknown if the horse was ever shipped to Brock. Brock never mentioned the horse in any of his correspondence, nor did anyone else who was close to him. There is no contemporary evidence that Brock rode Alfred to the battle or that he even owned a horse by that name. The entire story of

Alfred's role in battle is probably a later concoction based on Craig's legacy.

What Were Brock's Last Words?

Two contemporary accounts published in Canadian newspapers just after the battle of Queenston Heights reported that as he lay dying Brock said, "Push on the York volunteers" or "Push on, brave York volunteers." Many years later another contemporary remembered him saying, "Push on, my boys!" Although he may have uttered words like these earlier in the battle, it is unlikely that he spoke them after he was shot. Captain John B. Glegg, Brock's aide-de-camp, told Brock's brother two days after the battle that his final words were "My fall must not be noticed or impede my brave companions from advancing to victory." This sounds like something that Glegg invented to ennoble Brock's death.

The account of George S. Jarvis, a fifteen-year-old volunteer with the 49th Regiment of Foot, rings truer. He was near Brock when he was hit and was probably the first person to reach him. When he asked Brock if he was badly hurt, Brock "placed his hand on his breast and made no reply, and slowly sunk down." Because Brock had sustained a chest wound that quickly filled his lungs with blood, he died almost immediately and probably did not say anything.

Who Killed Brock?

Several Americans claimed credit for firing the fatal shot that killed Brock. The only credible claim was made by Robert Walcot, who told his story to a Philadelphia newspaper in 1880. Walcot said he saw Brock leading his men in a counterattack at Queenston. Being a good marksman, he borrowed a musket from an infantryman and rammed home a second ball on top of the first already in the barrel. He then took aim at Brock, fired, and watched the British general fall. Walcot's account is includes many details that add to its verisimilitude, and his testimony closely matches the report of George Jarvis, who watched Brock go down. Walcot's account is also consistent with the location of the entrance and exit holes made by the bullet in the coat worn by Brock that day.

Nevertheless, there are several problems with Walcot's story. The veteran was in poor health and close to one hundred years old when he told this tale, and although almost seventy years had elapsed since the incident, he had never before mentioned the subject, at least publicly. Moreover, even though Walcot remembered serving extensively in the war (evidently in the militia as well as the regular army), there is no record of his service. Although it is possible that Walcot killed Brock, the evidence is inconclusive. This is not surprising. In the fog of war, it is often difficult to pin down responsibility for any given death.

A contemporary account of the American assault on Fort George in 1813 sheds light on Walcot's claim. When an American sharpshooter was asked by an officer if he had hit every man he aimed at, he replied, "Yes, sir, all that I took aim at went down when I fired, but perhaps some of the other boys put them down, as they were all shooting as fast as they could load." Moreover, one man he had aimed at actually fell before he had a chance to fire. "If I had shot at that instant I would have thought that I had killed him when in fact it was some other one."

Such is the stress of close combat and the frailty of the human memory that postwar accounts of battlefield experiences—especially those like Walcot's, rendered long after the fact—have to be treated with considerable skepticism.

Where Did Brock Fall?

In 1860 a cenotaph was erected to mark the spot where Brock was killed. The project was probably hurried so that it would be ready for dedication when the Prince of Wales arrived for a visit later that year. The cenotaph is located on level ground at the south end of the town of Queenston. At the time of his death, Brock was leading a charge to retake the redan battery on the hillside, which a detachment of American soldiers under Captain John E. Wool had captured. It seems unlikely that any of the Americans defending the battery would have been far enough down the escarpment to hit someone standing where the cenotaph is located. Moreover, George Jarvis witnessed the fatal event and reported that Brock was shot, not on level ground, but as "he led the way up the mountain at double quick time." Thus it is unlikely that Brock was killed where the cenotaph is located. He probably fell near marker #4 in the Parks Canada tour, which is located about 200 yards southeast of the cenotaph up the escarpment.

Brock's Well-Traveled Remains

Despite all the mythology that has grown up around Major General Brock, one story is true: his remains are well traveled. Brock had the rare distinction of being buried four times. Although he was already well regarded in 1812, Brock's success at Detroit, combined with his heroic death at Queenston, transformed him into a genuine Canadian hero.

Initially, the deceased major general and his provincial aid-de-camp, Lieutenant Colonel John Macdonell (who was also killed at Queenston Heights), were buried in a bastion, then known as the York Battery, in the northeast corner of Fort George, some six miles north of where Brock had fallen. A participant called the funeral ceremony "the grandest and most solemn…that has ever been seen in Upper Canada." The remains of the fallen heroes were not disturbed during the American occupation of the fort in 1813.

In 1824 a monument was built on Queenston Heights to honour Brock, and the remains of the two men were reinterred in a vault under the base of the structure. The circular memorial was 135 feet high and contained a winding deck on top. At the time, it was the tallest memorial in North America.

In 1840, an attempt was made—possibly by an Irish-born anti-British terrorist named Benjamin Lett—to blow up the monument. Most of the crown was blown off, the staircase was destroyed, and deep cracks appeared in the main structure. At a public meeting, the monument's builder, an engineer named Francis Hall, claimed that he could repair the structure for £370, but others present thought the damage was too extensive and wanted to build a new monument. The monument was left standing until 1853, when it was demolished. It took three charges of explosives to do the job, which suggests that perhaps Hall was right. Before the demolition, the remains of Brock and Macdonell were temporarily buried for a third time in a private cemetery at Willowbank, an estate in Queenston belonging to the prominent Hamilton family.

A second, more impressive monument was completed on the Heights in 1853. Capped by a sixteen-foot statue of Brock, the structure is 185 feet tall. A staircase inside the column (now closed to the public for safety reasons) provides access to an enclosed observation deck below the statue. It was then the second tallest memorial of its kind in the world, after Christopher Wren's 202-foot column commemorating the Great Fire of London in 1666. The remains of Brock and Macdonell were reinterred in the base of the monument in the fall of 1853. This was their fourth and final resting place.

The Brock monument still commands the surrounding countryside. It is an impressive reminder of Brock's sacrifice in the War of 1812 and of Canadian patriotism and independence. It is also one of the most visible links that Canadians have today to the War of 1812.

*The second monument honoring Major General Brock was erected on Queenston Heights in the 1850s after the first was destroyed. (Lossing, **Pictorial Field-Book of the War of 1812**). Source: author's personal notes*

A small battle a few days before the big battle at the Heights took place on the Niagara River with the capture of the brig *Caledonia* and the brig *Pontiac*. The first built was the sloop *Pontiac* and the second built was the brig *Pontiac* shortly after. The brig *Pontiac* was captured in the battle on Lake Erie and taken to port on the U.S. shore. After the war it was scuttled, refloated, and outfitted, then sold to a group from Buffalo, where it sat as a victory war trophy.

References

Part 1 was taken from *The Canadian History Book*.

Many of these myths started in 1855 by means of newspapers on both sides of the border. But who shot Brock and the story of Alfred the horse had to have been started by the U.S. soldiers and added on to by our Canadian papers.